This Prayer Journal
Belongs to:

_____

DOMINIQUE OKONKWO

REMAIN
in the
VINE

A 10-Week Daily
Devotional
Prayer Journal
on the Fruit of
the Spirit

Contents

Love - Week 1

Joy - Week 2

Peace - Week 3

Contents

Contents

Faithfulness— Week 7

Gentleness – Week 8

Self-Control – Week 9

Contents

Fruit Salad - Week 10

Bonus Content

Introduction

How do we develop the *Fruit of the Spirit*? Once a seed of faith is planted, what does it take to produce its fruit? And what does fruit have to do with the Holy Spirit anyway? As I have gotten older, I spend more time reading food nutrition labels than ever. I realized that my diet profoundly impacts my physical health and overall wellness. I examine labels for additives and ingredients that disagree with my body and try to avoid them at all costs. As you will discover through these devotionals, the best thing about growing spiritual fruit is indulging in them later. No portion control is needed for these healthy fruits, and there are no nutrition labels to read.

Similarly, Paul, the apostle of Christ, tried to warn the Christians in Galatia about how to best maintain their spiritual health. He writes a prison epistle to the church on what it means to bear spiritual fruit instead of gratifying the desires of sinful nature. "But the fruit of the Spirit is love, joy, peace, patience, kindness, goodness, faithfulness, gentleness, and self-control. Against such things, there is no law (Galatians 5:22-23)." His letter supports what the apostle John wrote in John 15:5, "Yes, I am the vine; you are the branches. Those who remain in me, and I in them, will produce much fruit. For apart from me you can do nothing." But how do we remain in the vine? Spending time with the Lord in his Word and in prayer keeps us aware of his will and purpose for our lives. Just like the planted fruit tree, its nutrition comes from the source. Only with God may we bear much fruit, unblemished and organic.

I love mangoes! They are my favorite fruit. One of the reasons I love mangoes so much is that they are seasonal, unlike many other fruits, forcing me to wait for the summer months to indulge in those sweet and succulent fruits. The thing about mangoes is that they can only grow in suitable environments, and a young mango tree can take 2-3 years to bear fruit. But once developed, you can count on the tree to deliver good fruit every summer if it has been properly cultivated. Like the mango tree, God desires us to bear good fruit consistently over time while he prunes our branches.

According to a 2009 European Journal of Social Psychology study, it takes 18 to 254 days for a person to form a new habit. The study also concluded that, on average, it takes 66 days for a new behavior to become automatic. *Remain in the Vine* is a collection of 70 devotions, complete with Scripture reading and journal prompts, designed to help you walk each day with the Lord. Study each Fruit of the Spirit (love, joy, peace, patience, kindness, goodness, faithfulness, gentleness, and self-control) to grow deeper in your relationship with God.

Over the next ten weeks, you will develop a daily habit of spending time with God as you study the Fruit of the Spirit. You can circle the day you have read the devotional and write the date at the top of the page. God confirms that apart from him, you can do nothing. God loves you, and he desires daily fellowship with you. Devote yourself to meditating on God's Word daily to remain in him. He is waiting for you.

Love

The Greatest Commandment

"And you must love the Lord your God with all your heart, all your soul, all your mind, and all your strength. The second is equally important: 'Love your neighbor as yourself.' No other commandment is greater than these." (Mark 12: 30-31)

There are more than ten commandants that we frequently visit in the Old Testament. The Torah (the first five books in the Bible, including Genesis, Exodus, Leviticus, Numbers, and Deuteronomy) contains a total of 613 commandments covering many aspects of daily life, including diet, personal appearance, and behavior. Out of all these commandments, why do you think Jesus later establishes these two as the greatest ones? A teacher of the law recognized that these two commandments are more important than all burnt offerings and sacrifices. Sometimes it is easier to complete tasks with our hands than to deal with matters of the heart. God wants our hearts.

I'm thankful for

_____

_____

_____

Journal Prompt

Are there any matters of the heart that you must confess to God today? What are they?

Prayer

_____

_____

_____

_____

_____

_____

_____

_____

_____

_____

_____

_____

_____

_____

_____

_____

_____

_____

Love: Mon Tue Wed Thu Fri Sat Sun: _____

That's Deep

**"Then Christ will make his home in your hearts as you
trust in him. Your roots will grow down into God's love
and keep you strong. And may you have the power to
understand, as all God's people should, how wide, how
long, how high, and how deep his love is. May you
experience the love of Christ, though it is too great to
understand fully. Then you will be made complete with
all the fullness of life and power that comes from God."
(Ephesians 3:17-19)**

In 2017, my family experienced Hurricane Irma in Florida. This
Category 4 storm passed through my city and left a graveyard of
trees behind. Since we retreated to my parent's house to wait out
the Hurricane, we arrived at our home to find trees uprooted all
over the neighborhood. Only the older, more mature trees had
been able to resist the hurricane-force winds and were left
standing tall where we left them. God's love is like this. Once we
understand the full measure of his love, we can withstand any
force. May we find comfort in the strength of God's love.

Blessings and prayers answered
_____

_____

Journal Prompt

What evidence have you seen in your life that God's love for you
is boundless?

Prayer

_____

_____

_____

_____

_____

_____

_____

_____

_____

_____

_____

_____

_____

_____

_____

_____

_____

Love One Another

"Don't just pretend to love others. Really love them. Hate what is wrong. Hold tightly to what is good. Love each other with genuine affection, and take delight in honoring each other."
(Romans 12:9-10)

We live in a world with so many different opinions and biases; finding another person who 100% shares your ideals, likes, and dislikes is impossible. We are human! Some people are harder to love. But God is asking us to try. Find that common ground and hold firmly to that. Above all else, we belong to the same spiritual Father and should treat each other as brothers and sisters. Just being cordial with one another can go a long way.

Things on my mind
_____
_____
_____

Journal Prompt

In what ways can you share your love with others today?

Prayer

_____

_____

_____

_____

_____

_____

_____

_____

_____

_____

_____

_____

_____

_____

_____

_____

_____

_____

_____

Love: Mon Tue Wed Thu Fri Sat Sun: _____

We Are Family

"We love because he first loved us. Whoever claims to love God yet hates a brother or sister is a liar. For whoever does not love their brother and sister, whom they have seen, cannot love God, whom they have not seen."
(1 John 4:19-20 NIV)

In other translations of this scripture, John refers to "brother and sister" as "a fellow believer." In essence, how can you hate anyone who loves God? Despite how bad we may think someone to be, God loves them anyway. Including those who don't love him. God sees a redeeming value in every one of us and wants us to view one another similarly.

I need guidance
_____
_____
_____

Journal Prompt

What prevents you from seeing people as God sees them and loving them accordingly?

Prayer

_____

_____

_____

_____

_____

_____

_____

_____

_____

_____

_____

_____

_____

_____

_____

_____

_____

_____

Serve One Another

"For the whole law can be summed up in this one command: "Love your neighbor as yourself." But if you are always biting and devouring one another, watch out! Beware of destroying one another."
(Galatians 5:14-15)

Misery loves company. When things are not going well in life, it can be easy to allow your frustrations and negative outlook to impact those around you. Crab mentality is a theory that describes the crab in a bucket phenomenon. A lone crab can easily climb out and escape a bucket. But when placed in a bucket with other crabs, they pull each other back down into the bucket, which will ultimately lead to their demise. Similar to our relationships with one another, it can be easy to pull others down when we are not doing our best. Let us not damage one another because of our moods. God warns us about such behavior.

I'm thankful for

_____

_____

_____

Journal Prompt

How do you serve and encourage others around you?

Prayer

_____

_____

_____

_____

_____

_____

_____

_____

_____

_____

_____

_____

_____

_____

_____

_____

_____

_____

_____

Love for Enemies

"If you love only those who love you, what reward is there for that? Even corrupt tax collectors do that much. If you are kind only to your friends, how are you different from anyone else? Even pagans do that."
(Matthew 5:46-47)

Imagine this. You are walking home one evening and are held at gunpoint by a robber. He snatches your necklace, demands your ring, and steals away with your purse. Now imagine that this robber goes a step further and takes your life. With your last breath, you pray for this thief and his salvation. Seem absurd? This compassion for and forgiveness of others is precisely what Christ had while being put to death on the cross by the same people he was trying to save. To live in God is to give ourselves to God and others just like Jesus did when he cried out, "Father, forgive them, for they don't know what they are doing." (Luke 23:34) right before he was put to death.

Blessings and prayers answered

_____

_____

_____

Journal Prompt

Who is difficult for you to love? How can you love that person better?

Prayer

_____

_____

_____

_____

_____

_____

_____

_____

_____

_____

_____

_____

_____

_____

_____

_____

_____

_____

_____

Love: Mon Tue Wed Thu Fri Sat Sun: _____

God's Love and Ours

"We know how much God loves us, and we have put our trust in his love. God is love, and all who live in love live in God, and God lives in them. And as we live in God, our love grows more perfect. So we will not be afraid on the day of judgment, but we can face him with confidence because we live like Jesus here in this world."
(1 John 4:16-17)

God instructs us to love our enemies and pray for those persecuting us. Come again? That driver who steals your parking space—love them. That co-worker who gossips about you—love them. That person who hurt deeply someone you love—love them. Even that family member who knows exactly what to say or do to make you angry—love them too. If our heavenly Father loves the righteous and the unrighteous alike, who are we to be selective with our love? God distributes his perfect love among us and empowers us through the Spirit to love others.

Things on my mind

_____

_____

_____

Journal Prompt

Take an audit of your current relationships. Are there any that are suffering? How can you grow the love in those relationships?

Prayer

_____

_____

_____

_____

_____

_____

_____

_____

_____

_____

_____

_____

_____

_____

_____

_____

_____

_____

_____

Prayer List

Prayer   Answered

_____   _____

_____   _____

_____   _____

_____   _____

_____   _____

_____   _____

_____   _____

_____   _____

_____   _____

_____   _____

_____   _____

_____   _____

Joy: Mon Tue Wed Thu Fri Sat Sun: _____

The Sun Will Come Out Tomorrow

"Weeping may last through the night, but joy comes with the morning."
(Psalm 30:5)

I find so much comfort in God's Word. I look back at all the times I was saddened and hopeless because of life's unexpected outcomes or when I was without joy and cried myself to sleep. I remember that things turned out OK in every situation. I made it through, I persevered, and I found joy again. Because of God's grace, we awake every morning with a fresh perspective. Life may not always be perfect, but our troublesome situations are not everlasting. We look forward to spending eternity with God forever.

I'm thankful for

_____

_____

_____

Journal Prompt

What are some things that bring you joy? How can you incorporate those things into your routines to help keep your spirits up?

Prayer

_____

_____

_____

_____

_____

_____

_____

_____

_____

_____

_____

_____

_____

_____

_____

_____

_____

_____

_____

Joy: Mon Tue Wed Thu Fri Sat Sun: _____

The Source

**"I pray that God, the source of hope, will fill you
completely with joy and peace because you trust in him.
Then you will overflow with confident hope through the
power of the Holy Spirit."
(Romans 15:13)**

What is hope? According to Merriam-Webster's dictionary, the
word hope carries as part of the definition "desire accompanied
by anticipation or expectation." There is an expectation that God
will fill us with the desires of our hearts so long as we continue to
trust in him. Only hope derived from our trust in God will wholly
fill us with joy and peace. So when you pray, pray in expectation
as you focus on the Lord because "there is surely a hope for you,
and your hope will not be cut off" (Proverbs 23:18 NIV).

Blessings and prayers answered

_____
_____
_____

Journal Prompt

Where does your hope come from? Is God the primary source of
your joy?

Prayer

_____

_____

_____

_____

_____

_____

_____

_____

_____

_____

_____

_____

_____

_____

_____

_____

_____

Praise the Lord

"But joyful are those who have the God of Israel as their helper, whose hope is in the Lord their God."
(Psalm 146:5)

In the New Living Translation of the Bible, the phrase "praise the Lord" is written 194 times, with about half of those times noted in the book of Psalms. Think of the psalms more like poetry that reveals the writer's most intimate encounters with God. As you read through the psalms, you can understand why God is given so much praise through the heartfelt journal entries of the authors. Psalm 146 clarifies that the Lord is worthy of praise and that we can find joy in his faithfulness. We often hope in the things and people we can see and forget how mighty a God we serve. God helps, protects, sustains, and frees us because he loves us. Praise the Lord!

Things on my mind

_____

_____

_____

Journal Prompt

Is praise for God part of your daily worship? Write down some of the things you can praise God for today.

Prayer

_____

_____

_____

_____

_____

_____

_____

_____

_____

_____

_____

_____

_____

_____

_____

_____

_____

_____

Give Thanks

"Always be joyful. Never stop praying. Be thankful in all circumstances, for this is God's will for you who belong to Christ Jesus."
(1 Thessalonians 5:16 -18)

Joy, prayer, and thanks. However you order it, God's will is for us to pursue these actions in increasing measures daily. If you lack joy, you can pray for more. Giving thanks to God for the blessings you have in your life, even if they feel few, can also increase your joy. If you place your prayers and thanks in front of God daily, you will experience the joy he has willed for your life.

I need guidance

_____

_____

_____

Journal Prompt

What are you giving thanks to God for today?

Prayer

_____

_____

_____

_____

_____

_____

_____

_____

_____

_____

_____

_____

_____

_____

_____

_____

_____

_____

_____

He Lives

"For you will not leave my soul among the dead or allow your Holy One to rot in the grave. You have shown me the way of life, and you will fill me with the joy of your presence."
(Acts 2:27-28)

The Apostle Peter addresses the crowd in Jerusalem right after they witness the Holy Spirit ascend on the 12 apostles at Pentecost. He reminds the people of what was prophesied about Jesus before his crucifixion and resurrection from the grave. Earlier psalmist also wrote that if there is sin in our hearts, God will not listen to our prayers or save us from death (see Psalm 66:18). Death couldn't keep its hold on Jesus, a cause for celebration. God promises never to abandon the faithful to the grave, and we can find joy in his promise.

I'm thankful for

_____

_____

_____

Journal Prompt

Peter urged the crowd to repent and be baptized for the forgiveness of their sins. What are some sins you need to confess to God today?

Prayer

_____

_____

_____

_____

_____

_____

_____

_____

_____

_____

_____

_____

_____

_____

_____

_____

_____

_____

_____

Cheer Up

"Why am I discouraged? Why is my heart so sad? I will put my hope in God! I will praise him again—my Savior and my God!"
(Psalm 43:5)

Depression and anxiety can come in many forms. This mood disorder affects how you feel, think, and behave and can lead to various emotional and physical problems. Many forms of depression can be treated medically, but when depression stems from a lack of purpose and is a result of despair, trusting in God and his promises can bring about joy and encouragement. Look at the suffering Job endured in the book of Job. He went from being angry with God and cursing the day of his birth to realizing that God is sovereign over everything and would see Job through his present suffering (see Job 42:2). Job's story ends with God blessing the latter part of his life more than the first because he trusted in God even though the reason for his hardship was beyond his understanding.

Blessings and prayers answered

_____

_____

_____

Journal Prompt

What hope in a new life do you have in God, and how do you praise him?

Prayer

_____

_____

_____

_____

_____

_____

_____

_____

_____

_____

_____

_____

_____

_____

_____

_____

_____

_____

Songs of Praise

"Sing to the Lord, for he has done glorious things; let this be known to all the world."
(Isaiah 12:5 NIV)

There was a time in my life when I wanted a career change. I was convinced I was no longer on the right career path and wanted to leave the technology industry for something more rewarding, like teaching. After months of interviewing for a competitive teaching program and making it to the last round of interviews, I was not selected for the program. I was devastated. Fast forward to today, I realized that it was a blessing in disguise that I did not receive that job. God put other opportunities in my path that I didn't know about back then. Despite your present situation, God is doing great things. We don't give him enough credit! We should praise God for every circumstance, including those situations that don't work out the way we planned.

Things on my mind

_____

_____

_____

Journal Prompt

What glorious things has God done for you? Thank God for all that he has done and will continue to do.

Prayer

_____

_____

_____

_____

_____

_____

_____

_____

_____

_____

_____

_____

_____

_____

_____

_____

_____

_____

_____

Prayer List

Prayer   Answered

_____   _____

_____   _____

_____   _____

_____   _____

_____   _____

_____   _____

_____   _____

_____   _____

_____   _____

_____   _____

_____   _____

_____   _____

Peace

Deeply Rooted

"But blessed is the one who trusts in the Lord, whose confidence is in him. They will be like a tree planted by the water that sends out its roots by the stream. It does not fear when heat comes; its leaves are always green. It has no worries in a year of drought and never fails to bear fruit." (Jeremiah 17:7-8 NIV)

I haven't had the best track record for keeping my house plants alive. My family would tell you that it's hit or miss when it comes to them. This one plant, a 4-foot Bird of Paradise, thrived for months and suddenly started to grow mold in and around its stems. I tried everything to get rid of the mold. I used a fungicide spray, water and vinegar mix, and whatever else the internet told me to use. But none of that worked. Eventually, for the safety of my home, I set the plant outside on the side of the house until I could figure out what to do next. Much to my surprise, the plant began to thrive! Returning to its natural habitat had brought my dying plant back to its healthy state. My plant received the constant hum of sun and rain that it needed to be revived again. Is our relationship with God this way?

I'm thankful for

_____

_____

Journal Prompt

Do you fixate yourself in an environment where you can be directly connected to the Father so that your 'leaves' are always green? Free from mold or decay? Where are you planted?

Prayer

_____

_____

_____

_____

_____

_____

_____

_____

_____

_____

_____

_____

_____

_____

_____

_____

_____

_____

Peace: *Mon Tue Wed Thu Fri Sat Sun:* _____

In His Image

"Make every effort to live in peace with everyone and to be holy; without holiness no one will see the Lord."
(Hebrews 12:14 NIV)

Can we produce holiness ourselves? In the original Greek translation of the word holiness, *hagiasmos*, the usage of this word emphasizes the *process* of making or becoming holy. Like a tree produces its fruit by the type of planted seeds, holiness is produced in us by the foundation of the Holy Spirit. In bearing God's image, we can grow good Fruit of the Spirit, like peace. Being set apart by the peace that God gives us will bring us closer to seeing the Lord as we focus on becoming more like him.

Blessings and prayers answered

_____

_____

_____

Journal Prompt

In what areas in your life can you emulate the peacefulness of Christ?

Prayer

_____

_____

_____

_____

_____

_____

_____

_____

_____

_____

_____

_____

_____

_____

_____

_____

_____

Supernatural Peace

"Don't worry about anything; instead, pray about everything. Tell God what you need, and thank him for all he has done. Then you will experience God's peace, which exceeds anything we can understand. His peace will guard your hearts and minds as you live in Christ Jesus." (Philippians 4:6-7)

I pray for an out-of-this-world peace. The type of peace that can only be described as supernatural. But God says that prayer and thanksgiving are the only ways to obtain this type of peace. Why should we be anxious about anything when we can share everything with God the Father? As God reminds us, "I am leaving you with a gift—peace of mind and heart. And the peace I give is a gift the world cannot give. So don't be troubled or afraid (John 14:27)."

Things on my mind

_____

_____

_____

Journal Prompt

God promises to grant us supernatural peace through prayer and thanksgiving. Do you believe him? Write down some of those things that you are worried about.

Prayer

_____

_____

_____

_____

_____

_____

_____

_____

_____

_____

_____

_____

_____

_____

_____

_____

_____

_____

_____

Peace: *Mon Tue Wed Thu Fri Sat Sun:* _____

Reap What You Sow

"But the wisdom from above is first of all pure. It is also peace loving, gentle at all times, and willing to yield to others. It is full of mercy and the fruit of good deeds. It shows no favoritism and is always sincere. And those who are peacemakers will plant seeds of peace and reap a harvest of righteousness."
(James 3:17-18)

Have you ever planted a seedling or a sapling? I've tried and failed. One reason for failing was that I had no idea how much care was needed for this young tree and for how long. Particularly when it came to watering it. Because of the lack of moisture in the ground, my poor tree did not survive. I got as much from the tree as I gave—apparently, not enough. Our relationships mirror this example. Nurture peace in your relationships and watch how they will bloom.

I need guidance

_____

_____

_____

Journal Prompt

How do you handle conflict in your relationships? Is your way more or less peaceful?

Prayer

_____

_____

_____

_____

_____

_____

_____

_____

_____

_____

_____

_____

_____

_____

_____

_____

_____

_____

Sanctuary

"Those who live in the shelter of the Most High will find rest in the shadow of the Almighty. This I declare about the Lord: He alone is my refuge, my place of safety; he is my God, and I trust him."
(Psalm 91:1-2)

Psalm 91 is often attributed to Moses, possibly written during his 40 years of wandering in the wilderness. He writes of dangers like hunters, fatal diseases, terrors, and wild animals, all of which highlight the fear and uncertainty of wandering. He recognizes that those who remain in God's presence, like a chick with a mother hen, would have peace and comfort under the protection of God's wings.

I'm thankful for

_____

_____

_____

Journal Prompt

Where do you go for refuge when facing trials and are not at peace? Does anything prevent you from seeking refuge with God?

Prayer

_____

_____

_____

_____

_____

_____

_____

_____

_____

_____

_____

_____

_____

_____

_____

_____

_____

_____

Peace and Harmony

"And let the peace that comes from Christ rule in your hearts. For as members of one body you are called to live in peace. And always be thankful".
(Colossians 3:15)

Momentary peace can come from many sources. You can find peace on vacation, when pampering yourself, and maybe even at home. But there is only one place where you can obtain everlasting peace. This type of peace can only come from Christ. If he reigns over your life and heart, it is easier to experience his peace as we lean on his precepts. It is even better to enjoy peace with the body of Christ. For this, we can always be thankful.

Blessings and prayers answered

_____

_____

_____

Journal Prompt

As you meditate on God's word today, write down some of the things you are thankful for.

Prayer

_____

_____

_____

_____

_____

_____

_____

_____

_____

_____

_____

_____

_____

_____

_____

_____

_____

_____

_____

Peace: Mon Tue Wed Thu Fri Sat Sun: _____

God Bless You

"Blessed are the peacemakers, for they will be called children of God."
(Matthew 5:9 NIV)

Helping others to find peace with God is no small feat. God asks us to do more than break up fights or mediate disagreements. He expects us to share the gospel's good news with others so that they are ultimately reconciled to him. The key to obtaining peace in our other relationships is first to possess peace with God. As it is written, "For God is not a God of disorder but of peace, as in all the meetings of God's holy people (1 Corinthians 14)."

Things on my mind

_____

_____

_____

Journal Prompt

Before seeking to help others obtain peace with God, we, too, need to work out those unreconciled relationships in our lives. What are some of your relationships that need restoration?

Prayer

_____

_____

_____

_____

_____

_____

_____

_____

_____

_____

_____

_____

_____

_____

_____

_____

_____

_____

_____

_____

Prayer List

Prayer   Answered

_____   _____

_____   _____

_____   _____

_____   _____

_____   _____

_____   _____

_____   _____

_____   _____

_____   _____

_____   _____

_____   _____

_____   _____

_____   _____

Nobody's Perfect

"Always be humble and gentle. Be patient with each other, making allowance for each other's faults because of your love."
(Ephesians 4:2)

One of the sayings you hear as a child is, *"When you point the finger at someone else, there are three pointing back at you."* As much as you want to pull your hair out when someone does something to you that you can't stand, remember that you are likely to evoke the same response from someone else. We must be patient and give each other grace for our faults and mistakes. God did.

I'm thankful for

_____

_____

_____

Journal Prompt

Practice makes perfect. What are some ways you can practice being more patient with others?

Prayer

_____

_____

_____

_____

_____

_____

_____

_____

_____

_____

_____

_____

_____

_____

_____

_____

_____

_____

God's Timing

"But they who trust in the Lord will find a new strength. They will soar high on wings like eagles. They will run and not grow weary. They will walk and not faint."
(Isaiah 40:31)

Other translations of this scripture use the words "wait" and "hope" in place of "trust" in the Lord, but the message remains the same. We are human! We get tired, pooped, and wiped out at times. But rest assured, when we trust, hope, and wait on the Lord, he will reenergize us and give us vitality. When we live apart from God, it is harder to trust in his promises (see Ephesians 2:12). It's not enough to will ourselves to be stronger. We need the resilience and patience only God can provide. God's timing is always better.

Blessings and prayers answered

_____
_____
_____

Journal Prompt

Is there any area of your life that has just about taken you out? Are you tired? Have you relied more on something or someone more than God's promises?

Prayer

_____

_____

_____

_____

_____

_____

_____

_____

_____

_____

_____

_____

_____

_____

_____

_____

_____

_____

_____

Patience: Mon Tue Wed Thu Fri Sat Sun: _____

Even When it Hurts

"Be joyful in hope, patient in affliction, faithful in prayer." (Romans 12:12 NIV)

Have you ever been to the emergency room? Checking into a front desk and waiting your turn in a fluorescently lit room. You wonder how long you must wait to see the doctor before being admitted into another room behind those preliminary double doors - only to wait a little bit longer? You know you'll receive relief from your misery, but you cannot get past the pain at that time. God says wait. Remember that his timing is unlike our own and that while we faithfully pray for relief during our affliction, even when it is unbearable, we will eventually receive joy in the hope we seek, whether in this life or the next.

Things on my mind

_____

_____

_____

Journal Prompt

Write your prayer to God to deliver you from a current hardship or grief. What might change in you if you instead asked God to deliver you *through* the pain instead of *from* it?

Prayer

_____

_____

_____

_____

_____

_____

_____

_____

_____

_____

_____

_____

_____

_____

_____

_____

_____

_____

Life is Not Fair

"Be still in the presence of the Lord, and wait patiently for him to act. Don't worry about evil people who prosper or fret about their wicked schemes."
(Psalm 37:7)

The prophet David urges us to refrain from anger because it only leads to evil. Yes, it is hard to stand by and watch people succeed in areas while being unrighteous. Life can seem unfair in that way. We must protect our salvation by not sinning in frustration and letting our anger get the best of us (see Ephesians 4:26). We can only control what is in our control. Only God can handle the rest. Our job is to wait patiently on the Lord in whatever circumstances.

I need guidance

_____

_____

_____

Journal Prompt

What circumstances do you need to present to God today that are outside your control?

Prayer

_____

_____

_____

_____

_____

_____

_____

_____

_____

_____

_____

_____

_____

_____

_____

_____

_____

_____

_____

_____

Trouble Doesn't Last Always

"Dear brothers and sisters, be patient as you wait for the Lord's return. Consider the farmers who patiently wait for the rains in the fall and in the spring. They eagerly look for the valuable harvest to ripen. You, too, must be patient. Take courage, for the coming of the Lord is near." (James 5:7-8)

The Apostle James wrote this letter to those oppressed at the time. He uses the earlier prophets and Job's blessings as examples of how to remain patient while suffering. Job was "blameless and upright; he feared God and shunned evil" (Job 1:1). But while being put to Satan's test with the death of his children, loss of his possessions, and physical affliction, Job remained pure and sincere in his prayers to God without seeking ulterior motives. It is easier to practice patience during hardship when you hope in God, believe in his promises, and have optimism for the future.

I'm thankful for

_____

_____

_____

Journal Prompt

Consider your current ordeal. What do your hope for as an outcome of that situation? Present your requests to God.

Prayer

_____

_____

_____

_____

_____

_____

_____

_____

_____

_____

_____

_____

_____

_____

_____

_____

_____

Time-out

"A hot-tempered person stirs up conflict, but the one who is patient calms a quarrel."
(Proverbs 15:18 NIV)

Take a deep breath. Calm down. I know. Easier said than done. Amid conflict, it is better to wait. Wait to speak, be heard, react, or respond. Sometimes we need to listen first and assess the situation to diffuse it. It's taken much practice, but I have learned to ask for a time-out when walking into an argument or disagreement. I exercise God's patience and go off to pray before reengaging in the conflict.

Blessings and prayers answered

_____

_____

_____

Journal Prompt

What steps can you take to avoid being the hot-tempered person in an argument?

Prayer

By Faith

"Such things were written in the Scriptures long ago to teach us. And the Scriptures give us hope and encouragement as we wait patiently for God's promises to be fulfilled."
(Romans 15:4)

God has provided many examples of Biblical heroes who have persevered by faith. By faith, Enoch was taken up to heaven without death. By faith, Sarah delivered a child despite being well past child-bearing age. By faith, Moses led the people of Israel through the Red Sea onto dry land. These heroes were not perfect, but they waited on God to fulfill his promises. Ultimately, we have hope for the future because of Jesus' resurrection from death.

Things on my mind

_____

_____

_____

Journal Prompt

By faith, what promise do you believe God will fulfill for you? How long are you willing to wait for it?

Prayer

_____

_____

_____

_____

_____

_____

_____

_____

_____

_____

_____

_____

_____

_____

_____

_____

_____

_____

Prayer List

Prayer   Answered

_____   _____

_____   _____

_____   _____

_____   _____

_____   _____

_____   _____

_____   _____

_____   _____

_____   _____

_____   _____

_____   _____

_____   _____

_____   _____

Rich in Mercy

"Blessed are the merciful, for they will be shown mercy."
(Matthew 5:7 NIV)

We can and have been saved by God's grace. In his abundance of mercy and grace, he repeatedly forgives us of our sins. This blessing calls us to live continually in the kindness that we have already received. It calls us to extend compassion and forgiveness to others above judgment. How often do you receive an email or ad urging you to claim your FREE gift? For marketing purposes, the emphasis on the word FREE may look nice but is redundant. By definition, a gift is a thing given willingly to someone without payment; a present that is free to the giftee once received. Give mercy freely as it has been shown to you by your Father in heaven.

I'm thankful for

_____

_____

_____

Journal Prompt

How is your grace and mercy towards others? How can you make improvements in this area of your life?

Prayer

_____

_____

_____

_____

_____

_____

_____

_____

_____

_____

_____

_____

_____

_____

_____

_____

_____

_____

Sharing is Caring

**"The generous will prosper; those who refresh others
will themselves be refreshed."
(Proverbs 11:25)**

To be kind is also to be generous. Since God created everything that exists and all creation belongs to him, whatever wealth we have accumulated is tied directly to God's blessing and does not belong solely to us. God expects that we honor him with our wealth, talents, and time by sharing our *firstfruits*—first and best of everything, in service to him. In doing so, we will receive refreshments from our kind acts.

Blessings and prayers answered

_____

_____

_____

Journal Prompt

In what ways do you honor God with your *firstfruits*?

Prayer

A Friend Like Jesus

"And I have been a constant example of how you can help those in need by working hard. You should remember the words of the Lord Jesus: 'It is more blessed to give than to receive."
(Acts 20:35 NIV)

I know a woman who is the most giving person. She is the first person to show up when you need help and the last person to leave. She considers others before herself and never hesitates to spend her last dollar to support someone else. She is both hospitable and sacrificial. She loves hard and cares deeply. To someone watching from the outside, she could seem like someone with something to prove. But to a believer, you recognize the kindness and compassion of someone living a life in Christ by the fruit that she produces. I continue to imitate her heart as the Scripture suggests to "Follow [her] example, as [she follows] the example of Christ" (1 Corinthians 11:1).

Things on my mind

_____

_____

_____

Journal Prompt

Do you know someone personally whose example of kindness you can follow? If not, this person, how can you be more like Jesus in these ways? What characteristics of his do you share? Which could you work on?

Prayer

_____

_____

_____

_____

_____

_____

_____

_____

_____

_____

_____

_____

_____

_____

_____

_____

_____

Be Kind

"Get rid of all bitterness, rage and anger, brawling and slander, along with every form of malice. Be kind and compassionate to one another, forgiving each other, just as in Christ God forgave you."
(Ephesians 4: 31-32 NIV)

Malice is defined as "the intention or desire to do evil," according to the Oxford dictionary. The Apostle Paul instructs us to eliminate any form of evil and replace our mindsets with kindness, compassion, and forgiveness. He again brings us to Christ as an example of how to treat one another. As Christ has been kind to us, we should practice kindness to others as a counterattack to sinning against one another.

I need guidance

_____

_____

_____

Journal Prompt

Have you recently experienced rage, anger, argumentativeness, or anything similar? What brought you into that situation, and how can you handle them better in the future?

Prayer

_____

_____

_____

_____

_____

_____

_____

_____

_____

_____

_____

_____

_____

_____

_____

_____

_____

_____

Building Up the Kingdom

"God has given each of you a gift from his great variety of spiritual gifts. Use them well to serve one another."
(1 Peter 4:10)

The book of Isaiah references wisdom, knowledge, and counsel as examples of the Holy Spirit's gifts. But the list doesn't stop there. 1 Corinthians highlights healers, helpers, and administrative skills. Whatever the gifts, the Apostle Paul encourages us to eagerly desire them (1 Corinthians 12:31), so we can use them to serve one another in God's Kingdom. I recently watched a seven-year-old scribbling circles on a piece of paper during a morning church service. She was busy writing. After service, I asked her what she drew, and I noticed that each circle on the page had the name of a body part (i.e., ear, eye, hand, etc.). She was challenged to draw Jesus as one body and many parts, as written in 1 Corinthians 12. We can easily do the same exercise for documenting spiritual gifts because there are many.

I'm thankful for

_____

_____

_____

Journal Prompt

What is your spiritual gift in the Kingdom, and how do you use it? If you are not sure about what your spiritual gifts are, ask God to make them clear to you.

Prayer

_____

_____

_____

_____

_____

_____

_____

_____

_____

_____

_____

_____

_____

_____

_____

_____

_____

_____

_____

_____

The Unmerciful Servant

"Then the king called in the man he had forgiven and said, 'You evil servant! I forgave you that tremendous debt because you pleaded with me. Shouldn't you have mercy on your fellow servant, just as I had mercy on you?' Then the angry king sent the man to prison to be tortured until he had paid his entire debt. "That's what my heavenly Father will do to you if you refuse to forgive your brothers and sisters from your heart."
(Matthew 18:32-35)

In this parable, the King's servant could not pay his debt and pleaded to the King for his family to be spared from being sold. Unfortunately, the servant was not willing to grant the same mercy to a fellow servant and was punished as a result. God sacrificed his Son, Jesus, as the ultimate pardon for the forgiveness of our sins. Our kindness and forgiveness to others should rival God's unlimited forgiveness of us.

Blessings and prayers answered

_____

_____

_____

Journal Prompt

Is there anyone you need to forgive who has sinned against you? Are there any sins that you need to confess to God for forgiveness?

Prayer

_____

_____

_____

_____

_____

_____

_____

_____

_____

_____

_____

_____

_____

_____

_____

_____

_____

_____

Try Tenderness

"And we urge you, brothers and sisters, warn those who are idle and disruptive, encourage the disheartened, help the weak, be patient with everyone. Make sure that nobody pays back wrong for wrong, but always strive to be kind to each other and to everyone else."
(1 Thessalonians 5:14-15 NIV)

The Apostle Paul instructs the Thessalonians to be kind to one another. But not just by any old acts of service. He is asking the church to exercise some TLC—tender love and care—for one another to encourage the church's spiritual growth in the Lord and correct immoral practices. By expressing your kindness towards others and positively shaping the hearts and minds of your brothers and sisters, they will know you are a disciple of the Lord because of your love and tenderness (see John 13:35).

Things on my mind

_____

_____

_____

Journal Prompt

Ask God for help to use TLC when dealing with others.

Prayer

_____

_____

_____

_____

_____

_____

_____

_____

_____

_____

_____

_____

_____

_____

_____

_____

_____

_____

_____

_____

Prayer List

Prayer	Answered

Add Salt

"Be wise in the way you act toward outsiders; make the most of every opportunity. Let your conversation be always full of grace, seasoned with salt, so that you may know how to answer everyone."
(Colossians 4:5-6 NIV)

What does it mean to have conversations *seasoned with salt*? When eating and wanting to improve the taste of your food, the first thing you reach for is salt. In the same way, God wants our conversations to leave a "good taste" for others. Salt is also used to preserve food. God wants us to keep positively influencing others by the good Fruit of the Spirit we produce so that his goodness may be evident to all.

I'm thankful for

_____

_____

_____

Journal Prompt

Think about your last few conversations with a non-believer. Did you use the opportunity to have a graceful conversation? Was your Fruit of the Spirit evident to them?

Prayer

_____

_____

_____

_____

_____

_____

_____

_____

_____

_____

_____

_____

_____

_____

_____

_____

_____

Do the Right Thing

"We who are strong ought to bear with the failings of the weak and not to please ourselves. We should help others do what is right and build them up in the Lord."
(Romans 15:1-2)

This passage is not talking about just helping your neighbor with their groceries. Those who are stronger in the faith ought to support those who are weaker in the faith. There is a freedom in understanding God's will and purpose for our lives that could be harder to grasp and understand for others. Merely flaunting your convictions and spiritual freedom is unhelpful. Christ came to seek and save us *all* through him. Let us not forget that we cannot boast about what we have done. Only because of God can we have righteousness, holiness, and redemption in him (see 1 Corinthians 1:26-29).

Blessings and prayers answered

_____

_____

_____

Journal Prompt

Would you rate yourself stronger or weaker in the faith? Who can you think of stronger than you that might be able to help you? Weaker, whom you could help?

Prayer

_____

_____

_____

_____

_____

_____

_____

_____

_____

_____

_____

_____

_____

_____

_____

_____

_____

_____

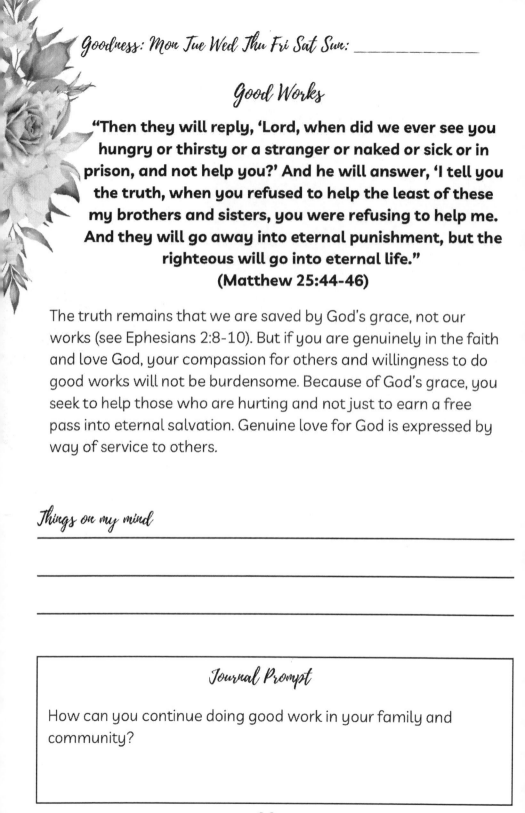

Good Works

**"Then they will reply, 'Lord, when did we ever see you hungry or thirsty or a stranger or naked or sick or in prison, and not help you?' And he will answer, 'I tell you the truth, when you refused to help the least of these my brothers and sisters, you were refusing to help me. And they will go away into eternal punishment, but the righteous will go into eternal life."
(Matthew 25:44-46)**

The truth remains that we are saved by God's grace, not our works (see Ephesians 2:8-10). But if you are genuinely in the faith and love God, your compassion for others and willingness to do good works will not be burdensome. Because of God's grace, you seek to help those who are hurting and not just to earn a free pass into eternal salvation. Genuine love for God is expressed by way of service to others.

Things on my mind

_____
_____
_____

Journal Prompt

How can you continue doing good work in your family and community?

Prayer

_____

_____

_____

_____

_____

_____

_____

_____

_____

_____

_____

_____

_____

_____

_____

_____

_____

Go and Do Likewise

"Then a despised Samaritan came along, and when he saw the man, he felt compassion for him. Going over to him, the Samaritan soothed his wounds with olive oil and wine and bandaged them. Then he put the man on his own donkey and took him to an inn, where he took care of him. The next day he handed the innkeeper two silver coins, telling him, 'Take care of this man. If his bill runs higher than this, I'll pay you the next time I'm here." (Luke 10:33- 35)

What do a priest, Levite, and Samaritan have in common? I know. It sounds like the beginning of a bad joke. In this parable, Jesus is trying to make a point about righteousness. All three men encountered a man who was beaten by robbers and left for dead. But the person who was despised above all because of their ethnicity was the most gracious and did not forsake the injured man. The Samaritan, who you would least likely expect, was the one who went above and beyond the call of righteousness. Regardless of your rank, title, status, or creed, everyone is called to be good.

I need guidance

_____

_____

Journal Prompt

Have you ever ignored God's call to help those less fortunate? In what ways can you support those who are less fortunate than you?

Prayer

_____

_____

_____

_____

_____

_____

_____

_____

_____

_____

_____

_____

_____

_____

_____

_____

_____

_____

_____

Excuses, Excuses

"Don't be fooled by those who say such things, for 'bad company corrupts good character.' Think carefully about what is right, and stop sinning. For to your shame I say that some of you don't know God at all."
(1 Corinthians 15:33-34)

Jesus *will* come again. Don't let others brainwash you into the YOLO (you only live once) theory. YOLO is all about selfishly living your life however you want, with no concern for others or the future, because this life is the only one you'll ever get. It can also explain why people sin because they believe there is no afterlife and no reward for good behavior. God promises that living a fruitful life in the Spirit is the way to live life to the fullest with God now and for eternity (see John 10:10).

I'm thankful for

_____

_____

_____

Journal Prompt

As you think carefully about what is right, are there any sins you need to confess to the Father?

Prayer

Code of Ethics

"May integrity and honesty protect me, for I put my hope in you."
(Psalm 25:21)

I almost stole a pack of water bottles once. It was an honest mistake. I walked out of the grocery store with a 24-pack of water bottles nestled in the bottom of my grocery cart. I was left with two options. I could load the groceries I did pay for, with the water bottles, into the back of my car and head home. Or I could trek back into the store with the water bottles in tow and pay for them. I did the latter. What is right is not always convenient, but how can we claim to be like Jesus if we don't value his principles in every situation? As cliché as the phrase may seem, when presented with a choice, as yourself, "What would Jesus do?"

Blessings and prayers answered

_____

_____

_____

Journal Prompt

Goodness is not always easy, but it is necessary to grow with Christ. What challenges have you faced concerning God's moral code?

Prayer

The Alabaster Jar

"But Jesus, aware of this, replied, "Why criticize this woman for doing such a good thing to me? You will always have the poor among you, but you will not always have me. She has poured this perfume on me to prepare my body for burial."
(Matthew 26:10-12)

Before this encounter, Jesus had already emphasized caring for the needs of the poor. So, imagine the resentment of onlookers when the woman poured out her expensive perfume onto Jesus when it could have been sold for profit and earnings given to the poor. Jesus reminded the disciples criticizing the woman that in helping to prepare his body for burial, as was the custom at the time, she was doing a good thing to honor God first with the best of what she had.

Things on my mind

_____

_____

_____

Journal Prompt

What has been your most significant sacrifice to serve and honor God? When have you let a desire to do good distract you from honoring God?

Prayer

_____

_____

_____

_____

_____

_____

_____

_____

_____

_____

_____

_____

_____

_____

_____

_____

_____

_____

Prayer List

Prayer	Answered

Faithfulness

By Faith, Not Sight

"And without faith it is impossible to please God, because anyone who comes to him must believe that he exists and that he rewards those who earnestly seek him."
(Hebrews 11:6 NIV)

Adults average 12-20 breaths per minute at a standard rate. It happens so frequently that we don't even realize that we are doing it until we are out of breath. Our spiritual life depends on our faith, as our physical life depends on the air we breathe. We don't count our breaths, but the atmosphere is always there and has never left us. Similarly, faith is our conduit to a faithful God who will never leave or forsake us.

I'm thankful for

_____

_____

_____

Journal Prompt

How has your faith in God been recently? Are you earnestly seeking him?

Prayer

Faith Over Fear

"The master was full of praise. 'Well done, my good and faithful servant. You have been faithful in handling this small amount, so now I will give you many more responsibilities. Let's celebrate together!"
(Matthew 25:21)

In this parable, the third servant did not rob, waste, or destroy the money he was given to invest. Yet he was reprimanded by his master because of his unfaithfulness to the task. He was asked to invest the talent that he was given but allowed fear to prompt him to hide it in the ground instead. God expects us to use whatever opportunities he provides and to have faith to use our gifts to make the most out of them.

Blessings and prayers answered

_____

_____

_____

Journal Prompt

The other two servants used the gifts their master had given them. How can you relate to either the servants who took advantage of their talents or the servant who hid his in the ground because of fear?

Prayer

Trust in Him

"This is the confidence we have in approaching God: that if we ask anything according to his will, he hears us. And if we know that he hears us—whatever we ask— we know that we have what we asked of him."
(1 John 5:14-15 NIV)

When you walk closely with God and produce good fruit, he grows your faith to know what to ask for, understanding that he will gladly provide whatever is best for you. It is like being an heiress to the wealthiest King in the world and being granted whatever your heart desires. We can be confident and trust God to keep his promises as we remain faithful to him. Let us not be tempted to demand from God the thing we *want* rather than to focus on the things we *need*. Trust that the Holy Spirit will work on your behalf while you seek God in prayer (see Romans 26-27).

Things on my mind

_____

_____

_____

Journal Prompt

Faithfully make your requests to God. Ask that *his* will be done.

Prayer

_____

_____

_____

_____

_____

_____

_____

_____

_____

_____

_____

_____

_____

_____

_____

_____

_____

_____

Bold Faith

"Then Jesus said to her, "Woman, you have great faith! Your request is granted." And her daughter was healed at that moment."
(Matthew 15:28 NIV)

Wow! What did this woman do to merit a response from Christ like this? Right before this verse, we learn more about this Canaanite woman who impressed God because of her bold faith. She refused to be dismissed until she could cry out to Jesus because she knew he was the answer to healing her demon-possessed daughter. Remember, God is not responsible for what Satan does because He is good (Psalm 100:5) and takes no pleasure in evil (Psalm 5:4).

I need guidance

_____

_____

_____

Journal Prompt

How does God feel about your faith? Do you boldly act out your faith daily, or do you only cry out to him when things are not going your way?

Prayer

Mustard Seed Faith

**"He replied, "Because you have so little faith. Truly I tell
you, if you have faith as small as a mustard seed, you
can say to this mountain, 'Move from here to there,' and
it will move. Nothing will be impossible for you."
(Matthew 17:20 NIV)**

Even the disciples who traveled with Jesus, and knew him
intimately, who witnessed his many miracles, struggled with their
faith. Mustard seeds are usually about 1 to 2 millimeters in
diameter. Tiny! When the disciples asked why they couldn't heal
the demon-possessed boy, Jesus said they didn't have faith that
they could. God can work with even the tiniest speck-sized
confidence when it's placed securely in him. He will grow our faith
more over time by proving himself repeatedly.

I'm thankful for

_____

_____

_____

Journal Prompt

Like Jesus' analogy, are there any mountain-sized circumstances
you are trying to move? How big is your faith that they will?

Prayer

God is Faithful

"The temptations in your life are no different from what others experience. And God is faithful. He will not allow the temptation to be more than you can stand. When you are tempted, he will show you a way out so that you can endure."
(1 Corinthians 10:13)

God is ultimately in control of all things. While James 1:13 teaches that God does not tempt us, we know that he is sovereign over the enemy. God will never allow us to be tempted beyond what we can bear. So why do we lose faith? We know that as we resist temptation, our faith grows. God is maturing our faith into completion so that we are not lacking in any areas in our life. We need not lose faith in ourselves.

Blessings and prayers answered

_____
_____
_____

Journal Prompt

What recent temptations have you experienced? How did God provide you a way out? Did you take it?

Prayer

_____

_____

_____

_____

_____

_____

_____

_____

_____

_____

_____

_____

_____

_____

_____

_____

_____

_____

Keep the Faith

"The faithful love of the Lord never ends! His mercies never cease. Great is his faithfulness; his mercies begin afresh each morning."
(Lamentations 3:22-23)

The prophet Jeremiah, also known as the weeping prophet, lived during one of the hardest times in Israel's history. He spent 40 years delivering God's message to the people of Judah. He witnessed his people endure war, captivity, and starvation while pleading with them to repent. They did not listen. Even during tough times, Jeremiah was a voice of hope because of his underlying faith in God. God never intended to abandon the people of Judah. He gave them several opportunities for redemption. "For I know the plans I have for you," says the Lord. "They are plans for good and not for disaster, to give you a future and a hope (Jeremiah 29:11)."

Things on my mind

_____

_____

_____

Journal Prompt

Jeremiah continued to serve God even though the people around him abandoned God. How are you willing to do the same?

Prayer

Prayer List

Prayer	Answered

Gentleness

Use Your Words

"A gentle answer turns away wrath, but a harsh word stirs up anger."
(Proverbs 15:1 NIV)

There are so many courses and trainings on navigating different kinds of conflict; marriage communication, strong-willed children, business relationships—the list goes on and on. God's Word sums up these topics in this one verse. Don't fight with fire. A fireman uses water to extinguish a flame. You, too, should use a gentler response in your conversations to avoid unnecessary conflict and soothe anger.

I'm thankful for

_____

_____

_____

Journal Prompt

How have your recent conversations been? Are your responses gentle enough to soothe anger or harsh enough to stir it up?

Prayer

_____

_____

_____

_____

_____

_____

_____

_____

_____

_____

_____

_____

_____

_____

_____

_____

_____

Forgiveness

"Make allowance for each other's faults, and forgive anyone who offends you. Remember, the Lord forgave you, so you must forgive others."
(Colossians 3:13)

Bear with each other and forgive one another. Surrender the thought of getting even and holding grudges. There is no limit on the number of times you extend mercy to others you may have resentment towards, even if that forgiveness has been given to the same person multiple times. Think about it; how many times has God forgiven you? If you're honest, the answer will be "more times than I can count." In Matthew 18, when Peter asked Jesus how many times they should forgive someone, Jesus responded 490 times (verse 22) which well exceeds the standard of the "3 strikes, and you're out" rule that is so prevalent in our society today. No matter the number of times, God's grace and mercy are unlimited. He has made us in his image so we can extend the same kind of forgiveness to others. So stop counting and forgive.

Blessings and prayers answered

_____

_____

_____

Journal Prompt

What allowances have you made to love others despite their faults? How can you both forgive and help those who have sinned against you?

Prayer

Common Ground

"To the weak I became weak, to win the weak. I have become all things to all people so that by all possible means I might save some."
(1 Corinthians 9:22 NIV)

As Christians, our standards are rooted in Christ and his Word. Unfortunately, many in this world do not share the same principles. As God's ambassadors, we must interact with all people to spread the gospel of Christ and establish them in the faith. As we encounter those with different convictions, finding common ground to forge relationships and ultimately win them to Christ is often necessary. We must be careful to handle others gently without violating the clear teachings of the Word of God.

Things on my mind

_____

_____

_____

Journal Prompt

In what ways can you help bring others closer to God? How can you tell the difference between convictions that can flex for the gospel's sake and those that cannot?

Prayer

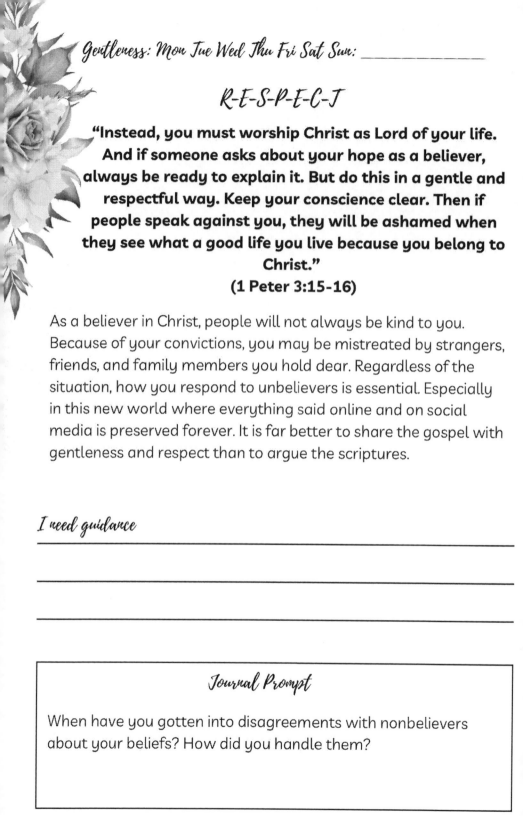

R-E-S-P-E-C-T

"Instead, you must worship Christ as Lord of your life. And if someone asks about your hope as a believer, always be ready to explain it. But do this in a gentle and respectful way. Keep your conscience clear. Then if people speak against you, they will be ashamed when they see what a good life you live because you belong to Christ."
(1 Peter 3:15-16)

As a believer in Christ, people will not always be kind to you. Because of your convictions, you may be mistreated by strangers, friends, and family members you hold dear. Regardless of the situation, how you respond to unbelievers is essential. Especially in this new world where everything said online and on social media is preserved forever. It is far better to share the gospel with gentleness and respect than to argue the scriptures.

I need guidance

_____

_____

_____

Journal Prompt

When have you gotten into disagreements with nonbelievers about your beliefs? How did you handle them?

Prayer

A Gentle Spirit

"Don't be concerned about the outward beauty of fancy hairstyles, expensive jewelry, or beautiful clothes. You should clothe yourselves instead with the beauty that comes from within, the unfading beauty of a gentle and quiet spirit, which is so precious to God."
(1 Peter 3:3-4)

Something marvelous happens when a woman gets a new hairstyle, some pampering, and wears a fancy outfit. As women, we can get so wrapped up in our outward appearance that we miss what God values in us most of all. In comparison, God prefers our inner beauty of a gentle and quiet spirit to our outward appearance. This beauty comes from the heart and will outlast all other forms.

I'm thankful for

_____

_____

_____

Journal Prompt

What does possessing a gentle and quiet spirit mean to you?

Prayer

Be Considerate

"Let your gentleness be evident to all. The Lord is near."
(Philippians 4:5 NIV)

I recall a conversation with a friend regarding what it means to be considerate. She is much older than I am and made a valid point: Nowadays, consideration for others is seemingly nonexistent in society and our homes. Merely saying, "excuse me," holding open a door, or even blessing someone after they sneeze, seems too much to ask of us. We have become a society so full of self that we have forgotten how important it is to be considerate of one another. Let us consider one other with kindness and gentleness as Christ has with us.

Blessings and prayers answered

_____

_____

_____

Journal Prompt

In what ways have you considered others above yourself?

Prayer

_____

_____

_____

_____

_____

_____

_____

_____

_____

_____

_____

_____

_____

_____

_____

_____

_____

_____

Stronger Than You Think

"Blessed are the meek, for they will inherit the earth."
(Matthew 5:5 NIV)

The Greek word for meek, *praus*, translates to "strength under control." In our Eastern worldview and culture, the concept of meekness is often looked down upon as a weak, spineless, spiritless way of being. Why would God allow such people to inherit the earth if that concept were correct? Only the strong can truly be meek. Meekness is the ability to show restraint and be calm and subdued even while provoked. It is complete and utter reliance on God's strength in all situations rather than oneself. To be meek is to be like Jesus.

Things on my mind

_____

_____

_____

Journal Prompt

Meek does not mean *weak*. In what ways will you continue to trust God in every situation?

Prayer

Prayer List

Prayer	Answered

Self-Control

Talk it Out

"If another believer sins against you, go privately and point out the offense. If the other person listens and confesses it, you have won that person back."
(Matthew 18:15)

Conflict in relationships is inevitable. Sure, it would be great if we never argued with one another, but that is not the reality. It can be easier to offer up your frustrations to someone else, but the Bible clarifies how we should work out our disagreements: Talk to one another first. Don't create a heightened situation by bringing others into the conflict prematurely. Talk it out to work it out. Refrain from broadcasting your issue as the first action you take.

I'm thankful for

_____

_____

_____

Journal Prompt

Do you need to work out any friction in your relationships with someone one-on-one? How do you plan to address the situation?

Prayer

Take A Chill Pill

**"Understand this, my dear brothers and sisters: You
must all be quick to listen, slow to speak, and slow to
get angry. Human anger does not produce the
righteousness God desires."
(James 1:19-20)**

Animosity, rage, hatred, annoyance, fury, impatience, and
violence derive from the initial anger that can take hold of our
emotions. Anger by itself is not a sin if it is directed against
injustice or evil. But if left unchecked, this emotion can damage
our attitudes and behaviors, making them unrighteous. Don't give
the devil a foothold by allowing such anger to be destructive and
controlling in your life.

Blessings and prayers answered

_____

_____

_____

Journal Prompt

How often do you get angry? Is this a consistent emotion in your
life? How can you practice being quick to listen and slow to
speak?

Prayer

The Company You Keep

"Oh, the joys of those who do not follow the advice of the wicked, or stand around with sinners, or join in with mockers. But they delight in the law of the Lord, meditating on it day and night. They are like trees planted along the riverbank, bearing fruit each season. Their leaves never wither, and they prosper in all they do." (Psalm 1:1-3)

"Birds of a feather flock together," as the saying goes. If you are consistently studying God's word, there is no need to take advice from people who are not. This is the stability we receive from God's word that we cannot obtain anywhere else. As you act according to his will, you will bear good fruit. Be careful not to conform to the lifestyles of non-believers as you invest in relationships with them. Don't ignore healthy boundaries that help you thrive spiritually.

Things on my mind

_____

_____

_____

Journal Prompt

As you take an inventory of your social circles, do any relationships need restraint? How often do you meditate on God's word?

Prayer

Turn the Other Cheek

"Don't repay evil for evil. Don't retaliate with insults when people insult you. Instead, pay them back with a blessing. That is what God has called you to do, and he will grant you his blessing."
(1 Peter 3:9)

Revenge is self-serving and is not of God. To be like him, we must ditch our old habits and submit to God's will. This includes the way we respond to persecution. It is natural to experience fight-or-flight reflexes when we feel mistreated. But God instructs us to abstain from sinning and bless one another with grace instead of mindlessly following instinct. God promises that just as no good act will go unrewarded; no evil deed will go unpunished. As Solomon said , "God will judge us for everything we do, including every secret thing, whether good or bad (Ecclesiastes 12:14)."

I need guidance

_____

_____

_____

Journal Prompt

What is your initial response when you have been mistreated? How can you bend that response to God's will?

Prayer

Grace Upon Grace

"Do not seek revenge or bear a grudge against anyone among your people, but love your neighbor as yourself. I am the Lord."
(Leviticus 19:18 NIV)

Cain held a grudge against his brother Able that resulted in him murdering Able (see Genesis 4:8). Esau held a grudge against his brother Jacob because of the blessing Jacob stole from him, so Esau plotted to kill Jacob (see Genesis 27:4). But Joseph, who was sold into slavery by his brothers, did not hold a grudge and was there for them when they needed him most (Genesis 50: 20-21). This is why loving your neighbor as yourself is the second greatest commandment. Hate leads to evil and the destruction of relationships. Like Joseph's, let our forgiveness be the key to a more purposeful life.

I'm thankful for

_____

_____

_____

Journal Prompt

Ask God to forgive our evildoing and those who do evil against us, as written in the Lord's Prayer (see Matthew 6: 9-13).

Prayer

Good Habits

"The end of the world is coming soon. Therefore, be earnest and disciplined in your prayers."
(1 Peter 4:7)

Be clear-minded and self-controlled when you pray. With all the dinging and pinging of our devices, it can be challenging to get the alone time with God we require. We need to establish regular habits for when and where we pray to combat the busyness of life. The Bible says that Christ will return unexpectedly like a thief in the night (see Matthew 24: 42-44). Since we don't know when Christ will return, we must be sober-minded and ready for when he does.

Blessings and prayers answered

_____

_____

_____

Journal Prompt

How is your prayer life? When and where do you pray most?

Prayer

_____

_____

_____

_____

_____

_____

_____

_____

_____

_____

_____

_____

_____

_____

_____

_____

_____

_____

Holy Living

"You used to do these things when your life was still part of this world. But now is the time to get rid of anger, rage, malicious behavior, slander, and dirty language." (Colossians 3:7-8)

On my 30th birthday, I had lunch at this cute little restaurant with about 15 friends. We laughed, we cried, and of course, we ate cake. I don't remember everything from that outing, but there was something a friend said to me that struck a chord. "You are a better person today than you have ever been," she said. And she was right. Despite my current challenges and imperfections, I was better. I am better. God has changed my life for the better, and I continue to be set apart from the unrighteousness and instability of my former life—day by day.

Things on my mind

_____

_____

_____

Journal Prompt

Where would you be without the Lord? How has he helped you to take better control of your life?

Prayer

_____

_____

_____

_____

_____

_____

_____

_____

_____

_____

_____

_____

_____

_____

_____

_____

_____

_____

Prayer List

Prayer	Answered

Fruit Salad

Pay it Forward

"As the Father has loved me, so have I loved you. Now remain in my love. If you keep my commands, you will remain in my love, just as I have kept my Father's commands and remain in his love."
(John 15: 9-10, 12 NIV)

Have you ever received a gift you weren't expecting? Jesus' sacrifice on the cross to suffer and die for our sins is the ultimate gift that was given to us freely. God commands us to love each other just as he has loved us. There is an unlimited supply of God's love. All he expects in return is for us to pay it forward and love one another generously. This is how we will remain in God's love.

I'm thankful for

_____

_____

_____

Journal Prompt

When is it easy for you to love others unconditionally? Who do you feel conditional love for or from?

Prayer

_____

_____

_____

_____

_____

_____

_____

_____

_____

_____

_____

_____

_____

_____

_____

_____

_____

Just Ask

"Until now you have not asked for anything in my name. Ask and you will receive, and your joy will be complete"
(John 16:24 NIV)

What does it mean to pray in Jesus' name? Coming to God in prayer is more about our posture and purpose than the actual words. When we approach God keeping his will and purpose in mind, we can expect God's power to work in our lives. "But if you remain in me and my words remain in you, you may ask for anything you want, and it will be granted! (John 15:7)" Only through pure and sincere prayer may our joy be complete.

Blessings and prayers answered

_____

_____

_____

Journal Prompt

Write your prayer for today in Jesus' name. Review your written prayers from the last nine weeks. Which of them are in line with Jesus' name? Are any not?

Prayer

Final Encouragement

"Finally, brothers and sisters, whatever is true, whatever is noble, whatever is right, whatever is pure, whatever is lovely, whatever is admirable—if anything is excellent or praiseworthy—think about such things. Whatever you have learned or received or heard from me, or seen in me—put it into practice. And the God of peace will be with you." (Philippians 4:8-9 NIV)

It can be easy to focus on the negative situations in our lives. Life can be unpredictable at times; you can come into some money unexpectedly or (perhaps more frequently) find yourself having to deal with unplanned expenses. Or, as you have finally found some peace and comfort in your life, you may be hit with some devastating grief. The Apostle Paul was writing this letter while held prisoner! Finding peace and tranquility in the middle of trials and chaos takes practice. And with Paul's example, we know that that kind of supernatural peace is attainable with preparation.

Things on my mind

_____

_____

_____

Journal Prompt

What circumstance are you currently dealing with that is not allowing you to be at peace? Today, consciously contemplate only the good things, as Paul describes.

Prayer

Wear Layers

"Therefore, as God's chosen people, holy and dearly loved, clothe yourselves with compassion, kindness, humility, gentleness and patience."
(Colossians 3:12 NIV)

We bear the image of Christ. God made us in his image, which is why he loves us so much. Regardless, we are fallen and still sin, so we must consciously put on the correct layers in our attitudes daily. To be like Christ is to exhibit the same forbearance he has shown us in our creation story and his ultimate sacrifice on the cross for our sins.

I need guidance

_____

_____

_____

Journal Prompt

Do you clothe yourself with the character traits of Christ each morning or the attitudes of the world? As outlined in the scripture, what qualities can you improve upon?

Prayer

Wait and See

"So let's not get tired of doing what is good. At just the right time we will reap a harvest of blessing if we don't give up." (Galatians 6:9 NIV)

I was in 1st grade, and my class was working on a science experiment. The goal was to plant our beans in egg cartridges before the winter break and see how much they have grown upon our return to school. Excitingly waiting to greet my beanstalk, I was frustrated to find out that I was the only student that didn't have any. After weeks of wondering why my bean hadn't sprouted, my teacher dug up my soil only to see that my beans had sprouted. Unbeknownst to me, I planted Asian bean sprouts that were wildly growing under the soil. I learned quickly that just because you don't see something happening doesn't mean it isn't. Plant good seeds, and they will grow.

I'm thankful for

_____

_____

_____

Journal Prompt

What seeds have you planted that you are waiting to harvest at the proper time?

Prayer

Faith and Endurance

"Dear brothers and sisters, when troubles of any kind come your way, consider it an opportunity for great joy. For you know that when your faith is tested, your endurance has a chance to grow. So let it grow, for when your endurance is fully developed, you will be perfect and complete, needing nothing."
(James 1:2-4)

Have you ever exercised after not working out for some time, only to suffer through muscle soreness and fatigue days afterward? Spoiler alert, if you don't exercise consistently, you will encounter morning-after pains every time. But after regular exercise, you start to appreciate the good pain that comes from knowing your body is getting stronger and building strength from all the workouts you've endured. Like our bodies, our faith can only be made stronger with resistance. We can find joy when we persevere through trials because we know that God is with us and he is in control.

Blessings and prayers answered

_____

_____

_____

Journal Prompt

Write your prayer for strength and endurance during trials and tribulations.

Prayer

Self-control: Mon Tue Wed Thu Fri Sat Sun: _____

Battle Training

"Finally, be strong in the Lord and in his mighty power. Put on the full armor of God, so that you can take your stand against the devil's schemes." (Ephesians 6:10-11 NIV)

The belt of truth, the breastplate of righteousness, the shield of faith, the helmet of salvation, and the sword of the Spirit, which is the Word of God, are all pieces that complete the armor of God in this Bible passage. God is not asking us to prepare for a physical battle but a spiritual one. Only spiritual armor will protect us from a spiritual attack, so it behooves us to train daily. Similar to Paul's athletic metaphor, to be the victor, you must endure rigorous training and self-discipline to defeat your opponent (see 1 Corinthians 9: 24-27). The armor of God is your protection. Wear it daily.

Things on my mind

_____

_____

_____

Journal Prompt

How are you preparing for spiritual battles?

Prayer

Bonus Content

And the Holy Spirit helps us in our weakness. For example, we don't know what God wants us to pray for. But the Holy Spirit prays for us with groanings that cannot be expressed in words.

Romans 8:26

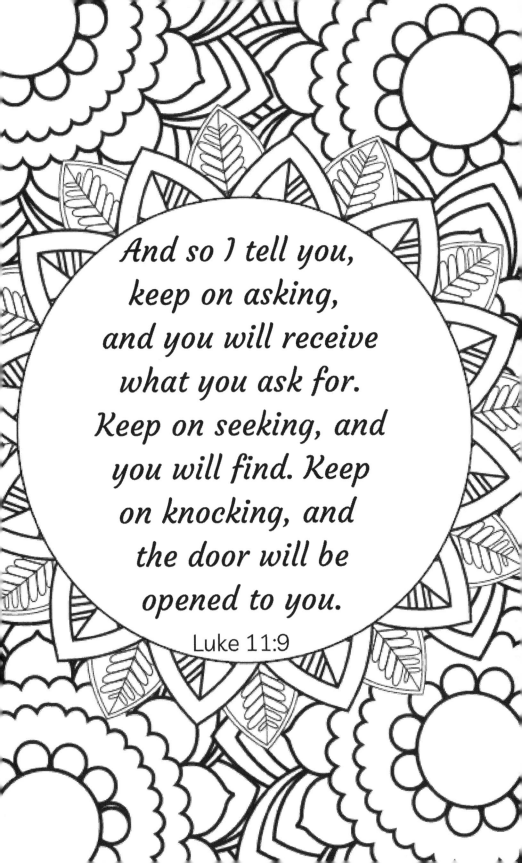

And so I tell you, keep on asking, and you will receive what you ask for. Keep on seeking, and you will find. Keep on knocking, and the door will be opened to you.

Luke 11:9

Great Prayers
of the Bible

- ☐ **Hannah's prayer of praise** - 1 Samuel 2:1-11
- ☐ **Morning prayer** - Psalm 5
- ☐ **Evening Prayer** - Psalm 4
- ☐ **The shepherd psalm** - Psalm 23
- ☐ **Praise and worship** - Psalm 24; 67; 92; 95-98; 100; 113
- ☐ **Guidance** - Psalm 25
- ☐ **Trust** - Psalm 37; 62
- ☐ **Deliverance** - Psalm 40; 116
- ☐ **Longing for God** - Psalm 27; 42; 63; 84
- ☐ **Forgiveness** - Psalm 51; 130
- ☐ **Thanksgiving** - Psalm 65; 111; 136
- ☐ **Help in trouble** - Psalm 66; 69; 86; 88; 102; 140; 143
- ☐ **God's constant love and care** - Psalm 89; 103; 107; 146
- ☐ **God's majesty and glory** - Psalm 8; 29; 93; 104
- ☐ **God's knowledge and presence** - Psalm 139
- ☐ **God's word** - Psalm 19; 119
- ☐ **God's protection** - Psalm 46; 91; 125
- ☐ **Prayers of Isiah** - Isiah 25; 33; 63-64
- ☐ **Hezekiah's prayer in his illness** - Isiah 38
- ☐ **Jonah's prayer** - Jonah 2
- ☐ **The Lord's Prayer** - Matthew 6:9-13; Luke 11:2-4
- ☐ **Mary's song of praise** -Luke 1; 46-56
- ☐ **Zechariah's prayer** - 1:68-79
- ☐ **Peter's thanksgiving** - 1 Peter 1:3-5
- ☐ **Paul's thanksgiving for God's comfort in trouble** - 2 Corinthians 1:3-4
- ☐ **Paul's thanksgiving for spiritual riches in Christ** - Ephesians 1: 8-14

Acknowledgments

I want to acknowledge the spiritual women in my life. Felecia for her unwavering commitment to the scriptures and unlimited support of my endeavors. Xiomara for encouraging me to start writing whatever God has put on my heart and for her unfailing love for God. Silvia and Kim for being the best examples of women's ministry leaders and their sacrificial love for the body of Christ. Ann for being a great example to me of remaining in the vine and the fruit that can produce in one's life as a result. Heather for impressing upon me early on as a young disciple the importance of knowing and studying my Bible daily. For all the women in our Princeton leadership group who never tire of meeting with one another and continue to live spiritual lives rooted in love. And so many other women in the One Miami Church ministry, like Shefeah, Dawn, and Blondy, who have supported me in my best and worst times. A special thanks go out to my book launch team for their early review of my book. And lastly, I would like to thank my mother for showing me how important it is to keep God first and foremost in my life.

Thank you for purchasing my book! Like this book? Please take a moment to share your review on Amazon and with family and friends. I truly appreciate you!

With all of my love,

Dominique

About the Author

Dominique Okonkwo is a Haitian-American award-winning author, wife, and mom of three who lives in Miami, FL. She is constantly inspired by her children and their many family adventures. She is passionate about publishing exceptional, inspirational literature that offers biblical encouragement to all. Her picture book series, *The Adventures of Super Obi*, stars an adventurous young boy with a trusty blankie who learns the lessons of life with the help of the Word of God.

Don't forget to download your FREE gifts! Visit dominiqueokonkwo.com and subscribe to her newsletter today. You can also follow her on Instagram and Facebook @MiamiMotherhood.

Made in United States
Orlando, FL
04 November 2022

24211643R00102